101 Tips For Youth Sports Officials has been compiled by Bob Still, National Association of Sports Officials, association development and public relations manager. It is an adaptation of the *Referee* magazine booklet *101 Tips For Better Officiating,* tailored especially to the needs of officials working youth sports.

Cover design and layout by Carrie Kwasniewski

Table of Contents

Introduction

One of the great things about sports is that no matter the level, the games are played basically the same way. The rules differ only slightly from the professional games to the youth leagues, and that's where the similarities end. Youth sports is about fun and learning skills, while professional sports is big business. Big business! Today, even collegiate and high school sports have become business first — fun second.

When talking about youth sports, it's vital to keep the word "fun" in the vocabulary. That's also important in officiating. I emphasize fun because that's a key component to successful officiating. If you're not enjoying yourself, you cannot expect to enjoy the game.

This book is a compilation of stories, shared experiences and tips from professional, collegiate, prep and youth league officials. It will help you become a better official. While most of the stories deal with high school, college and professional game incidents, you can learn from the experiences shared by the officials.

I know the original work developed by the editors of *Referee* magazine, *101 Tips For Better Officiating*, helps me each time I walk on any field. I keep a copy in my equipment bag and often refer to it prior to a game. I hope you will find this version of 101 Tips as helpful.

Just for the record, there are more than 101 tips between these covers!

Best wishes in your officiating pursuits.

Bob Still

Bob Still, Association Development and Public Relations Manager, National Association of Sports Officials

Chapter 1

Kindergarten's Five 'Golden Rules' Still Apply

Picture a typical kindergarten class: crayons, pony-tailed girls and finger paintings. That age of wonder for children is a time for learning lessons about life.

Just before a kindergarten class is ready to depart to cross the street to play, teacher Ms. Larson lectures the kids: "Before we leave, find a 'buddy' and pair off. Stay with your 'buddy' at all times because, as I've told you before, there's safety in numbers. Make sure you look both ways before crossing the street. Zip up your coats and don't dilly-dally. Tommy! Don't sass back!" With that, the children are off to play.

Little did you know back then that those kindergarten "golden rules" would be relevant today, including when we officiate.

STAY WITH YOUR BUDDY ...
THERE'S SAFETY IN NUMBERS.

Any time you officiate, it's a good idea to think about your crewmates. There are many times when at least two people should be present while performing a duty. Walk with your partners from the lockerroom to the game site. When the game ends, walk with your partners off the court or field. With at least two of you together, you can look out for each other and for potential problems. Emotions often escalate after games and occasionally people will try to confront you. With two of you together, you have a potential peacemaker and a potential witness if anything should go awry.

Taking that a step further, always walk together from your lockerroom to your cars.

Again, you may have some unexpected "guests" ready to offer their thoughts about your perceived lack of officiating ability. Ms. Larson was right. There is safety in numbers.

LOOK BOTH WAYS BEFORE
CROSSING THE STREET.

When walking to or from the field or court, visually scan the area to observe what's nearby; don't just put your head down and barrel through a crowd. With two officials looking around, you have a better chance of avoiding trouble.

ZIP UP YOUR COATS.

Look and dress as if you belong on the field or court. Appearance counts when you seek the respect of players and coaches.

Properly wear your uniform. If your jacket has a zipper, pull it up to a normal, comfortable height. If you have button shirts, button them up as you would a normal shirt. There's no need to have half your buttons undone or roll up your short sleeves to "show off." A clean, properly worn uniform will help you look the part, which can lead coaches, players and fans to accept your judgment calls.

> **Always walk together from your lockerroom to your cars.**

DON'T DILLYDALLY.

It is important to keep your games moving. That doesn't mean you should rush through things and skip important officiating processes. However, you should let the game establish a rhythm and then make adjustments if necessary.

Those who play, coach and watch the games we officiate want to see action. If a game is flowing smoothly, don't interrupt the flow for something that can be handled later.

Here's an example related to baseball: First pitch, swing and a miss for strike one. Next pitch, called strike two. Now, the plate umpire realizes there are tiny specs of dirt on the plate and he stops the game to brush off the plate.

What was his mistake? He ruined the flow of the game for something that could have waited until later. Once the game has found an acceptable rhythm, there's no need to interrupt that rhythm unless circumstances change.

DON'T SASS BACK!

Most officials get in major jams when they say things that are better left unspoken. While at times it's difficult to keep your emotions in check and not respond to comments from players and coaches, often it's best to simply ignore what they say. When a player or coach becomes profane or vulgar toward you, fight the urge to snap back. Just eject him and soon the storm will pass.

Of course, that's much easier said than done. But if you snap back you lower yourself to his standards; that usually creates more problems than it solves. As a result, you lose his respect and your own self-respect. You cannot afford to take things personally. Remember, most of the time they are not yelling at you, they are yelling at the uniform you wear and what it represents.

When contemplating your approach to the game, think carefully about the simple lessons you learned years ago when you were in kindergarten.

— Adapted from an original work by Bill Topp, *Referee* editor

Chapter 2

How to Master Any Sport's Rulebook

The rulebook is an official's bible. It provides the "nuts and bolts" basics which each official must master before he steps onto the playing surface. Rules knowledge and understanding are essential ingredients in a well-rounded official.

The problem is that most rulebooks are written more like legal texts than novels, making them tough to read and difficult to understand. Plus, related sections are often separated, forcing officials to hopscotch through various parts of the book and amass several references to find just one answer.

A major problem for youth-sport officials is "local rules." Almost every program has subtle alterations to the basic sport rulebook. You must be aware of the variations and ready to apply them before the game begins. Some of the biggest problems occur when officials don't know the local rules.

While other aspects of officiating are critical, solid rules knowledge and understanding form the root system from which an official will branch out, grow and prosper. Regardless of the sport or level you officiate, here are some tips that will help you move closer to mastering the rulebook.

SPEED-READ THE ENTIRE BOOK.

Read through the book as if you're cruising through a novel. You will not remember everything you read, but don't worry about that now. Familiarize yourself with different sections so you don't need to rely on the index.

CATEGORIZE THE RULES.

Some rules have more game-to-game impact than others. For example, the "equipment and court specifications" rule, often near the front of the book, is not necessarily one you should memorize first. While important, it is not the most important for someone who is trying to learn the rules. Ask yourself, what's more important: a basketball player's legal-guarding position or the radius of the jump-ball circle?

Read the "good" book in the following order: (1) Definitions. Mastering the definitions not only helps you on the court or field, it helps you study the rest of the book. (2) Live ball, dead ball. (3) Other game-specific chapters, such as out of bounds, pitching, kicks, etc. (4) Fouls and penalties. (5) Violations and penalties. (6) Scoring and timing regulations. (7) Players and substitutions. (8) Officials and their duties. (9) Court and equipment. (10) Rule changes, points of emphasis.

CHAPTER BREAKDOWN.

Now the real studying begins. There are many options, including:

• For each sentence, visualize several plays that relate to what's discussed. That helps take what you've read and applies it to real-game situations.

• Create a quiz. Read a sentence in the rulebook, then write it down without looking at the book. If you've correctly written the core of the sentence, write two related true-false questions, with correct answers and rule references. Move to the next sentence. Quiz writing aids memory retention and provides an effective preseason or pregame review.

> ## Ask yourself, what's more important: a basketball player's legal-guarding position or the radius of the jump-ball circle?

- Have several copies of the same rulebook. For convenience, have more than one copy of each rulebook. Keep them wherever you spend a great deal of time, such as in your living room, bedroom, bathroom, office, etc. That way, one copy is always accessible when time permits.
- Read in short increments of time. After the initial reading of the entire rulebook, study in increments of 15-20 minutes per sitting. Digest the material in bite-sized pieces.
- Review the book each day. Read some part of the rulebook each day, including during the offseason. Make it as much a part of your daily routine as brushing your teeth. Said Red Cashion, retired NFL referee: "I don't like a day to go by, not during the season but during the year, where I don't spend at least 15 minutes looking at that book."
- Study just before falling asleep. *USA Today* once reported that a study proved memory retention is enhanced by studying right before sleeping. Instead of watching TV as you begin to fall asleep, read the rulebook.
- Check related casebook plays. Once you've grasped a rule, read related casebooks and manuals before moving to the next rule. Casebooks enhance knowledge by taking rules and placing them into game situations. However, the casebook cannot replace the rulebook. Also, take quizzes and tests, which reinforce what you already know or emphasize what you don't know.
- Talk with rule experts. Attend local association meetings and confide in a few "experts." Those meetings often entail vigorous rules discussions that can be helpful. Note: Don't always take the local guru's words as gospel. If you're not sure about a ruling, look

> ## "I don't like a day to go by, not during the season but during the year, where I don't spend at least 15 minutes looking at that book."

it up, talk to your "experts" and find an answer. On occasion, local veterans apply incorrect rulings, which are passed on to the next generation of officials. Don't get caught in the loop.

Finally, remember the old saying, "Just when I thought I knew it all..." Said Cashion before retiring at the end of the 1996 season: "I study the rules a whole lot more now than I did before. After 39 years of officiating, I found out there is so much more I didn't know."

— By the editors of *Referee* magazine

Chapter 3

To Be or Not to Be!

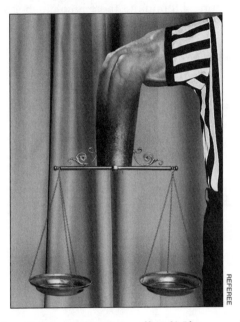

Do you want to be all you can be as an official? If so, consider the following tips from four veteran officials and referees' supervisors.

Youth sports officiating is unlike any other officiating experience you may ever encounter. At times the fans can be more ruthless than in any professional game. Let's face it — when children are playing, the fans are not uninvolved members of the community paying for "entertainment." These crowds are family, and as ridiculous as it may seem, the performance pressures parents place on themselves and their children often cause irrational behavior.

Some say professional baseball umpires have it easy. They're 30 feet or more from the fans, they have police protection all around and the stadiums have ushers to observe crowd behavior. The average youth league game has no police protection, maybe a screen and fence surrounding the field and absolutely no one policing the parents other than the parents!

That is why it is so important that your officiating be competent and professional. The image you present as you step on the field or court is your first opportunity to impress the coaches, players and fans. If they believe you know what you're doing, they begin to relax. If they suspect you're unsure or incompetent, they'll be restless and more likely to focus on your performance instead of the game.

For you right now, what is important is being a good official for your youth sports program. You may only be doing tee ball, but the game is as important to those children as the game on the other diamond between 13-and 14-year-olds. The perspectives are completely different, but playing the game is still important. Keep a simple focus: The game you are doing at the moment is the most important game being played.

Most officials share a common goal of moving up the ladder to work bigger and better games. Yet the higher you climb, the narrower the ladder becomes, making each successive upward step more treacherous than the previous one: One slip and the fall can be devastating. To enhance the odds of keeping your footing, here are 10 things you must be.

BE APPROACHABLE

Nobody likes to be ignored. One thing that turns off coaches and players is when an official seems unapproachable, standoffish, even cold. You can be great with rules and mechanics, but if your ability isn't tempered with human-relations skills your career will be fraught with problems.

Former NFL side judge Don Wedge retired following the 1995 season. He is also an ex-major college men's basketball referee. He states that the best official he ever worked with in the NFL was retired umpire Lou Palazzi. "He was a great official, had a way with the players and with other officials," noted Wedge. "He had a demeanor about him that calmed down everybody. ... When somebody would start to blow his stack, Lou in a very quiet and

> The average youth league game has no police protection, maybe a screen and fence surrounding the field and absolutely no one policing the parents other than the parents!

unassuming way was always there and able to take control. "

The same techniques worked on Palazzi's crewmates when they became confused or flustered. "I've been in games with (Palazzi) when the most unusual things would happen and the referee would start to stammer for the answer. Lou was calm and cool as he'd walk in and say, 'Well, maybe we ought to look at it from this way or that way."

Patty Broderick, a major college women's basketball referee and a supervisor of women's basketball officials, said there's "a real fine line" between an official being self-confident and being cocky. Noted Broderick: "I think cocky is, 'That's the call I made so sit down, coach, and I don't want to hear any more.' I don't try to put coaches on the defensive or try to intimidate them. I don't tell them to 'sit down and shut up!' I'm diplomatic. My style is easy-going. I'm pleasant, have fun. They know I'm a professional, but at the same time I'm human: I'm not beyond making mistakes. It's all human relations: I relate well to the coaches and players, yet at the same time am authoritative and direct: I'm in control out there and have lots of confidence."

BE PREPARED

No matter how long you've refereed or how many times you've worked with the same officials, it's crucial to have a pregame conference before every game.

"How can you referee without having a pregame?" asked John Moreau, a major college men's basketball referee. "I don't care if you refereed 20 games with (your partner) already this season, you've got to refresh your memory some. You've got to make sure everybody feels at ease."

Moreau elaborated: "I want to make sure we have things covered if there's a double whistle or an out-of-bounds play the calling official doesn't see. I don't want to wonder if you're going to call it; I want to know you're going to call it." Moreau said working a game without first having a pregame is akin to a teacher "going into a classroom without a lesson plan." He added that an official's "mental approach to the game is so important. If you don't have a

> "If you don't have a pregame, how can you be mentally ready to work?"

pregame, how can you be mentally ready to work?"

In youth sports, you'll often work with a new partner. Take time before the game to talk about each official's responsibilities — who is watching what. Regardless of the level, you should meet off the field at least 15 minutes prior to the start of your game to go over mechanics, local ground rules and any special interpretations or concerns about the teams involved. Don't leave doubts unresolved with your partner.

Verle Sorgen is the Pac-10 Conference supervisor of football officials. He worked football in the league for 20 years, mostly as a referee. He explained that a split-crew assignment, in which a game is worked by officials from two conferences, can pose major problems in terms of what each official expects from the other. The same problem can arise at any level of play when officials haven't worked with each other.

Said Sorgen: "When the game is being worked by a solid crew from one conference, you're used to each other, used to expecting them to be in certain positions because all that's been gone over in your clinic." That isn't necessarily true in split-crew games because not all conference supervisors preach identical mechanics, which is what Sorgen said "might have accounted for the problem" in a 1988 early-season UCLA-Nebraska game worked by a split crew from the Pac-10 and Big 12 (then known as the Big Eight).

"Nebraska intercepted a pass and 40 million people (national TV audience) saw the interceptor slip to one knee, stand up holding the ball over his head and run toward his team's sideline. Suddenly he realized nobody blew a whistle. He turned up field and trotted 60 yards for a touchdown. It was the slowest touchdown I've ever seen. We just missed it."

Sorgen said that after the play, Pac-10 referee Jim Sprenger asked each crew member for help. "Nobody could help so we were stuck. Nobody saw him go down. I don't see how that can happen, why nobody saw it. ..." That leads to the next tip:

BE READY

At times, it's the routine things that can trip officials.

In that same 1988 UCLA-Nebraska football game, a penalty was marked off improperly and the error went undetected by the officials. "It was a 15-yard penalty which was marked off 18 yards," said Sorgen. "That bothered me more than the other one because we have checks and balances on marking off penalties."

> # The game you are doing at the moment is the most important game being played.

The same season a Pac-10 crew committed a gaffe during the Oregon State-California contest. "We played an extra minute," noted Sorgen. "The clock flipped back and we didn't catch it. The bright spot was that it happened early in the season and woke up our guys real fast. As a result, we found and corrected timing errors at eight other Pac-10 schools that season."

BE FOCUSED

In order to do a solid job, you must maintain concentration through thick and thin. To do that, you cannot allow anything or anybody to get under your skin. That internal battle was fought by Patty Broderick during her early years of working basketball. "It was tough for me to get used to people yelling at me," said Broderick, "but that also taught me to tune out what they had to say."

At the time, there were few women officials, which posed a challenge for Broderick. "We (women) weren't supposed to know how to officiate. ... All of that toughened me up. At first I wore my feelings on my shirt sleeves, but I learned to adjust and put those feelings into my pocket. I'd bite my tongue when somebody said I was blind, even though I wanted to say something back to them. Gradually it got easier ... to ignore their comments."

BE YOURSELF

Due in part to the National Federation's and the NCAA's increased emphasis on uniform mechanics and signaling, some officials focus too much on how they make calls and how and where they stand, in the process losing sight of the game itself and what must be called. Said Don Wedge: "Yes, uniform mechanics are good, but you can't take the individual personalities out of the thing completely."

Although he hasn't worked a basketball game since 1980, what he sees at the major college level disturbs him. "I'm observing robots, which is what the powers want," said Wedge. "But those robot officials have forgotten what they're out there to do, which is to control the game first and foremost, and to administer it within the framework of the rules.

"Today's officials are ... too worried about some guy who's sitting in the stands or some coach who's going to report them. ... Just go out and work.

BE SURE

John Moreau said his greatest fear is "making a 'phantom call' at the end of a game. I know every call is important, but to call something that's not there ... at a critical time would be devastating." To do that, an official has to think about the game and how he fits into it. Knee-jerk reactions are ill-conceived. "I have a common-sense philosophy that ... the best call is a good no-call," said Moreau, "and it's not who is right, but what is right that's important."

As a youth official, you're there to ensure the safety of the players as well as make sure the game is played fairly by both sides. At times you may make the wrong call (we're all human and it happens), but there may be times when you can correct yourself without making a major production out of it. Do what is right for the game and for both teams. You may not please everyone at the moment, but if you consistently do what is right you will eventually earn the respect of both teams.

Moreau said that a few years ago he worked ACC games with an official who was prone to making poor calls at important stages of games. "He consistently made phantom calls toward the ends of games. There was a pattern." Fortunately, Moreau said, that official didn't last long. "His schedule went from top-quality to minimal to now, where he's out of officiating."

BE REALISTIC

Your officiating chums might think you're crazy for turning down a promotion, but that's what you should do if you're really not ready to move to the next-higher level.

Remember, if you move up too soon, you may forever eliminate the chance of another try.

The need for officials in youth sports (as well as other levels) is great. If you succeed as a good youth official, there will be

> Maintain concentration through thick and thin.

> ...you're there to ensure the safety of the players as well as make sure the game is played fairly by both sides.

opportunity to work high school junior varsity and varsity level games — if you want.

For example, with the growth of women's college basketball has come the need for more female officials. "If a guy doesn't work for me, he'll have a chance to work somewhere else; the woman might be limited," said Patty Broderick, supervisor of women's basketball refs for both the Big Ten and Midwestern Collegiate conferences. She added that if equally qualified male and female refs vied for the same roster spot, Broderick would select the female.

While that type of "affirmative action" provides more opportunities for female officials, there are inherent risks that some women may be pushed ahead too quickly. Broderick acknowledged that has occurred and said, "I'm not a proponent of doing that. We have to educate our women officials to be ready; if they don't have the qualifications, don't take the jobs."

Your opportunities in youth sports will vary — sometimes during the same day. It is not uncommon for a youth official to work a tee ball game and then do a 9- to 10-year-old baseball game. But keep your focus. Remember, with each level increase the game becomes more competitive and the skill levels improve.

BE BALANCED

While gaining experience by working a slew of games is helpful, it's possible to call too many games. When your officiating glass is full, whatever water you pour into it spills wastefully over the top.

It's counterproductive to work too many games or to work games at levels which don't offer challenges.

Patty Broderick said that as she moved up the ladder, her most difficult transition was weaning herself from high school basketball. Typically she would work a prep game on Friday night, a small college game another night and then a couple of Division I games a few nights later. The combination of all those games created a problem. Explained Broderick: "At times I'd make high school calls in college games and vice versa. If I'd just had a college game, I'd

It's counterproductive to work too many games...

call the high school game too loose. Finally I told myself I had to call one or the other because I wasn't getting any better. That's when I decided to quit high school and concentrate on college."

BE SAVVY

Knowing the rules is an initial step toward becoming a capable official. The next step: To understand the rules. Noted Verle Sorgen: "I don't think rules knowledge per se is what we're looking for as much as rules understanding, which follows rules knowledge. It's relatively easy to officiate strictly by the rules, but that's not what we're looking for in the Pac-10 and in college football in general. We're looking for officials to apply the spirit and intent of the rules."

John Moreau related a situation that underscores Sorgen's point. Moreau said that with four seconds to play in a small college game and team B ahead by one point, team A, which was not in the bonus, had a throw-in from its backcourt. "B's coach told his kids to overplay on defense and foul if necessary to prevent A from taking any kind of shot."

As A1 dribbled, he was fouled just before the game-ending horn sounded. "B's coach knew he'd won because A wasn't in the bonus," continued Moreau. "But as he was walking over to shake hands with A's coach, in the background he heard: 'Personal foul on black 32. Two shots, intentional foul.' The guy made both free throws (and team A won)."

Moreau was appalled when he saw that play on videotape. "There's no way on God's green Earth that was (an intentional) foul. To top it off, after the game that coach told me A's coach said, 'You know I'd like to beat you any way I can, but not like that.' It's obstacles like that we all have to overcome."

BE BETTER

Complacency can be an official's worst enemy. No matter what you've done lately and no matter how lofty your reputation, you must firmly believe that you can become an even better official.

Patty Broderick whistled six consecutive NCAA Division I

> ## You must firmly believe that you can become an even better official.

women's basketball Final Fours (1987-92), including five title games. But she refuses to rest on her laurels, in the process setting a positive example for others. "I may have it made," said Broderick while the streak was intact, "but there's no slacking off because now the heat's on; I have to perform to maintain an image and that's just as tough as trying to build an image. I'm judged by a different standard now."

Broderick said for that reason, "I have to work even harder. I'm in the limelight and have to prove it wasn't a fluke, not just to those around me but to myself. I have to prove to myself that I deserved everything I got and there may be a smidgen of self-doubt in there. I guess I like to see things in black and white: You could call me a doubting Thomas. I do like to see the end result, but I know it will come because I won't quit until it does."

Some days you may feel you worked a perfect game. When that happens, take time to remember what you did right. It might never happen again. Remember the reasons behind the calls and learn from them every time.

Think about creating a checklist to go over after every game. Ask yourself questions such as, "Did I hustle between plays? Did I smile and look like I was having fun? Did I keep the game moving so everyone felt involved? Did I give my best? Did the kids and the coaches have a good time?"

If you can answer "yes" to those questions, you've done your job well. It's time to move on to the next game, the next challenge. If not, then ask yourself more in-depth questions that address your motivation; your purpose and role. Think about your answers and then strive to improve.

— Adapted from an original work by Tom Hammill, Racine, Wis.

> ## Did the kids and the coaches have a good time?

Chapter 4

Is it Who You Know or What You Know?

Politics is a nasty word to most officials. They believe that knowing the right people will help them move up the officiating ladder. Is that perception accurate or is it just sour grapes? What can you do, without compromising your principles, to enhance your chances of upward mobility? This story cuts through the myths to examine the political realities of officiating.

You've seen it happen. The oldest referee in your association, who also happens to be the president, gets the biggest game of the year. The association secretary is selected to handle a clinic (and pick up a nice speaking fee at the same time). Someone in the group who "can't ref his way out of a wet paper bag" is hired by a college conference.

Unfortunately, politics exist in every segment of youth sports. Parents try to influence the selection of their child to a certain team; coaches try to influence officials during specific games or manipulate officiating assignments.

> Youth leagues exist for the kids they serve.
> If a league forgets that and gets caught up
> in political back-biting, it will ultimately fail.

Youth leagues exist for the kids they serve. If a league forgets that and gets caught up in political back-biting, it will ultimately fail. As you develop your officiating, consider whether the league you're working is right for you. It probably is not if it's fraught with political problems.

Why do those things happen? Most officials offer a simple, one-word answer: Politics! Then they'll add: "Politics are everywhere!"

True or false?

• Politics are largely responsible for which officials work the best schedules and the most prestigious games.

• Politics are responsible for which officials handle rating decisions and hold leadership positions within an association.

Answers to both: True. But there is more to politics than the negative image so often the topic of angry conversations among officials.

Check Webster's. You'll find some interesting words used to define "politics." Crafty. Unscrupulous. Cunning. If you think of politics as people taking shortcuts, the lazy official looking for a quick road to the top of the officiating list, those words ring true. On the other hand, another Webster's definition describes a totally different side of politics: "... wise; prudent in devising and pursuing measures; shrewd; diplomatic." It's the more attractive side of politics, now frequently called "networking."

Both definitions are accurate. Your own experiences determine which you feel is more dominant. Those same experiences probably determine if politics and networking have enhanced your career.

To find out how different officials view politics, and how they use politics, we discussed the subject with several active rank-and-file referees and umpires from around the country. The common denominator: Officials relate politics to "career advancement."

"Young officials need to be taught that politics is real in the officiating world," said Paul Wilson, of Norman, Okla. The former NASO board chair is the director of recreational services and an instructor at the University of Oklahoma in Norman. Wilson officiated at the major college level for more than eight years. Today, he concentrates on basketball only and officiates at the small college and high school level in order to be closer to work and home. A confessed "officiating junkie," in his younger days, Wilson's officiating career has at various times included baseball, football, track and swimming.

His is the negative view of politics, including any number of ethically questionable activities he's witnessed over the years designed to ingratiate one person to someone with the authority to promote a career. Personal favors, complimentary meals, coerced social activities, well, you get the point.

But Wilson agrees that new officials, or officials who want to advance their careers, must do something to gain recognition. "In the real world, politics are very nasty. As a nation we see politicking as, 'You have to give up something to get something.' You owe somebody something at the end of the whole political sequence," explained Wilson. "If you are 'networking' you are putting your information, your tools, your skills in front of the right people. Those people, if they have integrity and any ethics, eventually are going to say: 'This is a person we need to use. He deserves a shot.' "

One example is Wilson's own experience in the Oklahoma Intercollegiate Conference of Officials, a group he joined in 1972, hoping to advance from high school to collegiate basketball games. "I spent five years in the conference before I even got a game," he remembers. "I realized then there were politics."

Wilson also remembers that several varsity coaches asked him to work JV contests. Two wondered aloud why he was not working varsity ball. Of course, Wilson was wondering too.

"What did I start doing?" he recalled. "I started figuring out from other officials where to hang out to get in 'the clique.' I started socializing in 'the circle' with the guys who were 'in' with the president of the association, with the assignor. All of a sudden I was networking the right people. All of a sudden I was starting to get some games. It took me five years before I figured it out. No matter how good I was and no matter that the collegiate coaches were saying they wanted me, I couldn't get games until I started playing politics."

> "I think the best way for a new official
> to move up is to learn the rules,
> learn the mechanics..."

LEARN THE POLITICAL PROCESS

There are several important steps for any official to take before attempting to advance, through politics or networking. The list reads like an introduction to officiating: Study the rules, perfect your mechanics, gain game experience, arrange availability. Then ...

"I think the best way for a new official to move up is to learn the rules, learn the mechanics, apply them and just do his job," said Dave Hughes, a marble carver and installer who works football in and around Woodbridge, Va. Hughes also thinks that under the right circumstances, a new member can take full advantage of opportunities within an association.

"If he's given a job, on the board of directors or something, do that job. A new guy won't make any political enemies when he's coming up if he studies hard and does his job." Hughes admits to making major political mistakes that haunted his career until he joined a new group of officials.

"When I was in my first officials' association," he recalled, "we had a clique: The top people. In my opinion they acted like (they were better than others) and I told them so. Naturally, that doesn't go over too well, so you don't progress. When I moved to the second association I just kept my mouth shut. I did my job to the best of my ability and let that pull me along."

Hughes credits the lessons learned during his first membership with helping him understand how to survive politically. In the new group, with his closed-mouth philosophy, he "went right to the top."

Did Dave Hughes compromise his principles by keeping his "mouth shut"? Not likely. Instead, Hughes applied a good dose of discretion, principles intact. He resorted to networking, making sure he introduced himself to the new association's leadership, explained his officiating background, offered his availability and stood by his ability. He worked a number of games "below" his accustomed level while the new group tested his competence. As his credibility grew, so did his schedule.

Dave Hughes committed serious political errors, but improved his standing by joining a new officials' group. That's impossible for many amateur referees, who are limited geographically. How can an

> "Generally, the people in charge like advice and constructive criticism..."

official salvage a career within an organization after digging himself a political hole?

"It depends on how he dug the hole," said Tony Thompson of Snellville, Ga. (near Atlanta). "If he dug the hole because he did not participate in the training sessions, take the rules exams or attend any of the meetings, then obviously the only way he can get back into good standing is to start the next season doing those things. Those can be the easy holes to dig out of, even though they can hold you back a year or two. If you dug your hole by interfering in the internal workings of a group, that sometimes can be a little tougher."

Thompson's point of view is based on experience: He works baseball football and basketball, and is co-owner of a trophy and award retail store. He's also the supervisor of baseball umpires for the Southeastern, Atlantic Coast and Southern conferences. Thompson makes it clear that if someone has a negative comment about the job he does, he expects to hear it first hand.

"It's obvious in this world that somebody has to be in charge," said Thompson. "Generally, the people in charge like advice and constructive criticism, but they don't like negative criticism about how they're doing their jobs, getting back to them. ... The best way is to go directly to the source and sit down and talk to him. I don't think there's an assignor or a supervisor anywhere in the country who won't take the time to talk."

What you do on the field can lead to as many problems as what you say off the field, even if your rules knowledge is solid and your mechanics reliable. That's true particularly if the "performance" steps across a line of conduct that's locally accepted and politically enforced.

In Reno, Nev., the basketball and football schedules of Butch Miller are not growing as fast as he'd like. Despite his goal of working major college, or even the pros, he admits having trouble filling a high school calendar. But he does not have trouble explaining why.

"Because of my personality," he says openly. "I'm very outgoing and able to wear a lamp shade on my head, so people don't (respond well to) me. I get this flippant, 'I'm better than they

> **"Heaven forbid you miss a call and it's in the paper."**

are' reputation. It's hurt my chances for moving up in my association."

According to Miller, a Reno firefighter, the problem is assignors and others who worry about his lack of conformity. Some of the comments he's heard include: "He's looking for attention"; "he does things people don't consider ordinary"; and "we don't want him in our group because he might show off."

At the same time, Miller is convinced it is important to develop a personal style. "If you don't have something that sets you apart," he said, "you're not going to make it."

Miller is struggling to develop his own style while he tries to fit in with other local officials. He says he's "looking for ways that the people who are on top got on top ... something that will help overcome whatever politics I'm going to encounter."

In New Orleans, baseball umpires face a unique political problem: There are three separate umpire organizations servicing various schools, leagues and levels of competition. Those groups allegedly have experienced rashes of political infighting.

"The politics determine what association works what league," claims Thommy Boesch of Metairie, La. He is director of management information systems for a local medical clinic and a member of one New Orleans umpires association. "The leagues play the associations against each other. There are personalities involved within the associations ... you can't combine them into one."

Typical business tactics, like underbidding game contracts, are present but constitute the least of the area's problems, said Boesch: "You have back-biting and finger-pointing. Heaven forbid you miss a call and it's in the paper. The other two organizations really try to take advantage of that.

"They'll go to a specific school and say, 'So and so blew this call; so and so blew that call. You really don't want that crew, you want our crew.' It's a real bad situation."

SIDESTEP THE NIGHTMARES

Avoiding political problems is difficult, even for a veteran official. Dave Hughes did it, but only after his career suffered the

> "...go out of your way to meet the people who are in positions of importance."

Let your job speak for itself.

setbacks imposed by political "enemies" he created for himself. The advice is simple: Attend meetings and games, work within the group's leadership structure, conform as best you can to the expectations of the group and carefully choose an officials' group if options are available.

The description from football official Dick Lindstrom, Green Bay, Wis., offers an appropriate summary: "If you're a good official and you want to get ahead, you go out of your way to meet the people who are in positions of importance."

Lindstrom's logic is glaring when you consider a simple game assignment. Said he: "When you have two people who are somewhat similar, close to equal, one you know and one you don't know, who are you going to go with? If you feel confident in someone, you're going to go with somebody you like."

Lindstrom, a 43-year-old elementary school counselor, is candid about his position on politics. He "detests" the negative aspects often associated with the word. That's because of his political experiences in local government: He served two-year concurrent terms on the Green Bay City Council and the Brown County Board of Supervisors before other obligations forced him out of public life. He feels an official who wants to get ahead, into the "inner circle," has to be willing to carefully invest time and effort.

"Make an attempt to get to know the people within 'the circle' without sacrificing your own standards and ethics," said Lindstrom. "If it means that I get to know somebody in our association because it might help me get games, I might do that. ... Does it mean I go out and drink beer with those guys all the time? I sure hope not. I don't believe in a lot of drinking. If I do that I'm sacrificing my beliefs. But if I go out with those guys because I want to go out with them, fine.

"When you look at the people in the 'inner circle,' they're the ones who have devoted the time and effort to be there," Lindstrom continued. "They've been the officers, they've volunteered to do training. A lot of the people out of the 'inner circle' complain about 'that group inside.' But look at the group: They are the people who are the movers and the shakers in the organization."

"Sometimes perception is reality," said Tony Thompson. "Sometimes the top officials stay together at the meetings and after

"...performance earns promotion."

the meetings because they're used to being around each other."
Social relationships are particularly important for officials working
in local associations. Those officials will often work together during
a season, many times for their entire careers. But as an official
advances to the collegiate level, association friendships become less
important.

"When you get into the higher levels," Thompson explained,
"members are from such a scattered geographical area that you
don't have but one meeting a year. It's not like your local group
where you meet once a week on Sunday and everybody can go to
the local Pizza Hut to sit together and talk."

BECOME A 'NETWORK TARGET'

As a college baseball supervisor, Thompson faces a constant
barrage of officiating contacts. Umpires from across the Southeast
call, write, even visit, hoping to be added to one of his three
conference baseball staffs. That presents few problems, according to
Thompson: "Contacts can be a great source for putting your name
on the table and giving you a shot at it. If you live in a town that's
not close to a metropolitan area you may never get known. If a
person has the abilities to be a good umpire or a good referee, I
don't see anything wrong with him asking me or another official to
help put him in contact with the right people. We do it in our jobs
every day. Nobody wants to stay where they are. Nobody's content
making $15,000 a year when with a job promotion he can make
$20,000. So long as you're qualified I see nothing wrong with
making professional contacts to enhance your career."

But an aspiring college official has to walk a fine line between
promoting himself and forcing himself on people who make hiring
decisions.

"I think once your name's in front of the people sometimes it's
best to leave well enough alone. Let your job speak for itself once
they're aware of who you are," said Thompson, endorsing the
"networking" concept. At the same time, he warned against a
common mistake: Evading proper channels in an attempt to be
hired.

"Ninety percent of our applicants contact the conference office
first," said Thompson, describing the accepted method of applying

to the Southeastern Conference (SEC). "They are put in touch with John Guthrie (associate commissioner), who gets their applications, sends them letters saying we have received their applications. It tells them what we need, what we expect from them and how we will be in contact with them in the future."

Thompson added that if aspiring SEC umps barraged the commissioner with phone calls at his home "they would get tremendously negative responses because they are trying to evade channels and sneak through the back door."

Whether you use networking or politics to advance your officiating career, you'll still need ability. Whether you're moving from grade school to frosh football, or from junior college to major college basketball, contacts lead to opportunities; performance earns promotion. At least that's the ideal situation.

"The officiating world is so ingrained with politics that quality doesn't always rise to the top," said Paul Wilson.

Amen, say most officials.

—Adapted from an original work by Scott Ehret, Appleton, Wis.

Chapter 5

Learning the Basics of Networking

"Networking is the process of expanding a base of contacts in business or any activity." In officiating, networking describes an effort designed to introduce an official (or crew of officials) to assignors, supervisors, athletic directors, members of an officiating organization and anyone else who might be a beneficial contact.

Although there are no "official" definitions, the consensus difference between networking and politics is the inherent or assumed level of integrity of each contact. Networking generally indicates a straightforward introduction, which ideally includes a summary of officiating experiences and availabilities. A political contact is widely assumed to include some promise of an exchange of favors, a "you scratch my back and I'll scratch yours" attitude.

Here are common steps to developing a network of officiating contacts:

- Learn the rules and mechanics of the game.
- Comply with local or state registration requirements.
- Join one or several local officials' associations.
- Introduce yourself to a wide variety of people in those associations.
- Be open. Seek opportunities to work as many games as possible.
- Explore local procedures to determine whether athletic directors or coaches are actively involved in assigning games (if so, you'll have to meet them).
- Encourage new acquaintances to introduce you to others involved in assigning games in your area.
- Follow-up each introduction with some tangible form of contact (phone call, letter, etc.).
- Insure that your tangible contact includes a brief summary of your officiating experience and your desire to work. Include your availability if possible.
- Be aggressive without being pushy.
- After you determine who handles assignments and who is responsible for filling "emergency" reassignments, don't be afraid to make an occasional courtesy call at a strategic time of day. Between 3:00 p.m. and 4:00 p.m. on game-day afternoons is a typical "crisis" time for assignors who have been stood up. If you can work that evening, calling the assignor may enhance your chances of being selected as a replacement. Even if there is no emergency that day, your call may be remembered.
- Be patient. Acceptance in officiating can be a slow process; in fact, it may never occur. That's the sad but simple truth.

> ## Join one or several local officials' associations.

Chapter 6

Despite officials' good intentions, sometimes fights do erupt. Still, there are many things you can and should do to identify and deal with problems that could lead to fights. No matter what sport or level you work, as an official your goals must include the firm commitment to do whatever it takes to...

Prevent the Explosion

REFEREE

Early in my football career, my crew was sent to a game between two neighboring towns far from where we lived. It was somewhat of a "plum" assignment for me, the neophyte, and I took it as an honor. We all figured that the schools wanted an "impartial" crew from as far away as possible since the game was the yearly skirmish of a noted rivalry.

The contest was indeed spirited and intense, but because the execution and contact were on such a high plane, we felt that we rose to the occasion and worked a crisp game. How crisp we learned later as we peeled off our uniforms in the lockerroom. The athletic director came in and said: "Boy, am I glad we got through that one all right. You fellows probably don't know what took place here this past week."

He was right, we had no clue and no one chose to inform us before we walked out onto the field, either. Turns out that the towns were basically in an uproar in the week leading to the game. Police had to be called out to chase groups of kids parading through the rival towns in bunches of souped-up cars, screaming insults. Each school's front steps were daubed with painted curses and the opposite school's logo. That's not all: One night, a 15-foot beechnut tree was planted at the home stadium's 50 yardline. What that was supposed to stand for no one could guess (during the coin flip, we had been mildly puzzled by that patch of new sod), other than the hint that perhaps one team was accused of being "beach nuts," as both towns were on a lake.

The most doleful act of all, however, was that one night the home coach's car was pushed out of his driveway, rolled down a hill and sunk in the lake. But we hadn't been told any of that. Whose strategy it was to keep us in the dark we'll never know. The gist of it was this, though: We took it to be a normal albeit vigorous game. Good staunch competition. And that's the way it turned out. I've often wondered how we'd have acted if we'd been programmed, eyes bugged out and all that. Needless to say, we had a brisk conversation with much cluck-clucking of tongues on the long drive home.

In part because the media "plays it up," today there seems to be abundant "extracurricular" violence in all major sports. For example, within a two-week period, three different NBA referees were physically assaulted during games. All three incidents were witnessed by national television audiences. Fines and suspensions followed each event and debates raged on sports-talk shows across the land. Several players were ejected from NFL games for "touching" officials. Lastly, there was the spitting incident in Major League Baseball on the last weekend of the 1996 regular season.

Not that long ago, on Sept. 25, 1993, a total of 21 players were ejected from five major college football games, including 12 players from the Colorado-Miami (Fla.) game alone.

Doug Harvey, a 31-year National League umpire who retired after the 1992 season, says that violence in sports "clearly is a reflection of society. You have drivers shooting each other; then you're gonna have moms and pops attacking Little League umpires. Many people evidently feel they can solve problems through physical retaliation." Much of that stems from defiance of authority (officials), which leads to flaring out at opponents during games.

Dick Schindler, the associate executive director and editor of the football and basketball rulebooks for the National Federation until his retirement in 1997, offered this disquieting viewpoint: "We (society) may not be telling (the athletes) it's wrong. In fact, in some instances and among certain groups, we may be asking them to actually suspend their normal behavior for two hours during a game. In some cases, that may be asking too much."

So, as an official, how do you deal with the escalating tendency toward violence in sports? From an informal "poll" I've taken among a variety of officials, there seems to be two contrasting approaches to the issue. One is to acknowledge upfront tension and potential antagonism, in effect trying to squelch outbursts before they occur. The other approach is to deliberately avoid focusing on them and instead develop a recognition strategy and a coping mechanism, all the while actively nurturing a positive climate throughout the contest.

Those who advocate advance warnings to players believe that it is foolhardy to go into a game without knowing the social-racial-ethnic composition of the contestants. It may be inner-city, blue-collar sons against country-club suburbanites, a Jewish-based institution versus a Catholic one, an elite private school against one composed mostly of minorities, or even two schools from the same district with nearly identical ethnic backgrounds. It may also be two adjoining towns with a history of keen competitiveness, often with one feeling inferior to the other. Swedes against Swedes could be more explosive than blacks versus whites.

Football official Jack Lutz of Dover, N.J., relates a personal example: "You have to know about your community and schools and the socioeconomic mix. We had a pair of blue-collar football teams, one basically Italian and the other Irish, many of them sons of immigrants. But two other morsels were also part of the stew: Both schools got toppled a week earlier, although each had been a solid favorite. Plus, a strike in the shipyards had recently idled a lot

> "Many people evidently feel they can solve problems through physical retaliation."

of Italian fathers. There was a heavy air of tension before the game.

"We warned them at the start that we'd tolerate no horseplay," continues Lutz. "But in the third quarter, two kids erupted in a verbal confrontation and both sides poured onto the field. Coaches weren't much help in the ensuing melee because they too went after one another with verbal barbs. (Finally), we got the teams settled; the ref notified both coaches that he'd terminate the game if another fight broke out. Consequently, the rest of the game was a drab affair, players just going through the motions to avoid another incident. The fight was the climax. It ruined a good game."

A football referee I recently worked with in a small college tilt began the pregame chat with the captains by saying: "Look here, we don't want any cheapshots, and no taunting either. ... "Should we officials begin games on such negative notes? Should we issue warnings based on assumptions and preconditioned expectations, such as common knowledge about a disruptive coach or players with bad-boy reputations? Sometimes no matter what you do you can't avoid problems.

Doug Brown, from Ipswich, England, recalled a time that at the coin toss a captain spit onto the ground and vowed, "We're going to run the ball down your goddamn throats, all of yuz!" Well, you certainly can't let that remark slip by without addressing it. Says Brown: "Our teams know each other so well that they talk almost constantly, and part of it is trying to establish a macho image. Of course, we get to know the troublemakers too and we talk them out of fouls away from the ball."

"We make it part of our pregame conference," says Chuck Piebes of Danbury, Conn. "We'll describe anticipatory clues to each other and we'll speak with coaches about rivalries or problems: 'We have information about past outbursts and we'll try to let you play. But we'll also exert our own efforts to maintain control if antagonisms surface.'"

Knowing the community, the schools, having a sense of history and recognizing the clues all are part of the read in anticipating outbursts of emotion that lead to fights. Sometimes there's no read to it, though, as in Doug Brown's case of a captain spewing threats. U.S. Federal Court judge Jack Bissell, of Newark, N.J., is also a prep

> "You have to know about your community and schools and the socioeconomic mix."

> # "Every time you see an unusual behavior, ask yourself why."

ice hockey official. He may have gotten to the heart of the issue when he asserted, "It's as simple as the advice your first-grade teacher gave you about crossing the street: Stop, look and listen."

Where does the stop come in? Each sport has its "dead spots," its pauses in the action. Right at that very initial pause is the point of potential volatility. A runner slides into second base and kicks the ball from the fielder's glove. That's the point to move in on the scene, so the runner can stand up and dust himself off right after you properly declare the ball dead: Be there. Just your presence may prevent retaliation.

Says Doug Harvey: "Every time you see an unusual behavior, ask yourself why. About a pitch possibly deliberately thrown at a batter: 'Did he have a reason to do that?' If those questions come to mind, then they must trigger a response, meaning march out there and warn the pitcher. Of course, you'll pull the manager out by your action, but tell him that you are basically protecting his players."

"The signs are so elementary in basketball that it would take a dunce to ignore them," says Jaime McCaig of Toronto. "Take the dunk. Who is enraged after a flamboyant dunk? Not the dunker, that's for sure. What message does the dunk carry? 'I'm pounding on you. See if you can take it!' and then we wonder why players get mad."

Jay Silver, from Indianapolis, offers a warning: "Sometimes it begins just by pointing and gesturing, without words being exchanged. Watch for eye contact when they line up for free throws."

McCaig offers additional advice: "If you have a severely rough play or a foul that's perceived as unnecessary, the instant you blow your whistle you better be moving right toward the cluster (of players). You dare not yet turn your head toward the scorer's table to report it. Get in there and 'head it off at the pass,' before the rumble." Stop when you sense it's necessary.

Jerry Seeman, NFL director of officiating, says that one of his "10 commandments" is, "Thou shalt be a great dead-ball official." He means that no one is simply staring at the dead ball spot once a play ends. All officials are to have their eyes roving, their heads sweeping. They get forward progress and out of bounds spots with their feet while taking in the action around them. "The physical presence alone is one deterrent, perhaps the prime one," insists Seeman. "But we also have 'The Accordion Effect' on all dead-ball fouls that prevent the snap and on all flare-ups after plays or after scores." That effect is when all officials begin to pinch-in from their fanned out positions, even if trouble does not actually erupt. "They back off if the coast is clear," says Seeman. "But they're on their toes, ready to sprint to the trouble if it ignites."

The stop in all dead-ball situations segues to the look mode for an alert official, because sometimes there are no sounds to grab his attention. Arnie Leisher of Chambersburg, Pa., tells of a football game in which one team clearly had in mind intimidation tactics when the players stuck out their chests toward opponents in confrontational posturing after each pileup. While rising, they also pushed down on the pile and nudged opponents with shoulders and elbows when returning to their huddle. Leisher stopped one linebacker in the act, after sizing him up as a leader, and told him: "You're too good to be doing that make-believe stuff." Later, after a resounding tackle, the same linebacker lifted his opponent to his feet, looked Leisher in the eyes and said, 'Is that better, ref?' " Hearing that story, Jack Muscalus, from Harrisburg, Pa., says that "it's best to appeal to their strong natures, their senses of pride of leadership."

Hank Nichols, NCAA coordinator of men's basketball officiating, says that sometimes officials are their own worst enemies. "Referees are at fault many times for ignoring inflammatory remarks. Warning people is a must," says Nichols. "Officials saying they won't be supported by the league office is a copout."

"It's a fault-finding world today," adds Merle Butler, ASA national director of umpires. "To combat the use of vulgar language, some local areas are taking action by banning certain well-defined obscenities, with offending teams penalized by calling out the next batter and so forth. People get fed up. Often the penalties are pretty harsh." Adds Ed Hochuli, an NFL referee from the Phoenix area, "When a kid loses his legs, he resorts to his mouth."

Referring to the football crew on which he works, Dave Kraft of Lombard, Ill., says: "We have a basic philosophy. First of all, a tone of efficiency and control are absolute watchwords. We have the

> **"Thou shalt be a great dead-ball official."**

> # "When a kid loses his legs, he resorts to his mouth."

responsibility to enforce the rules. Piling on and late hits are forbidden." Continues Kraft, also a baseball umpire: "In baseball, as soon as a batter is hit by a pitch, I instantly step between him and the pitcher and/or catcher. Just being there will prevent the malarkey. In both sports, let them know they can talk only to their teammates. We're not having a gabfest out there."

Kraft echoes the views of others when he declares: "Many supposedly good officials simply do not recognize escalating tension. Continually focusing on the progress spot (football), pivoting away from players when you call a foul (basketball) or dipping your head after a harsh tag (baseball, softball) lead you to ignore action after plays. Being oblivious to the triggering mechanism is worse than ignoring it. It's sinful."

Jack Muscalus adds that at times it takes experience to recognize that trouble is brewing. "You have to distinguish between normal banter and veiled threats," says Muscalus. "I've learned to stop and cock my head, which means my ears are attuned, and just consciously force myself to listen. We have to recognize that the natural human tendency in reacting to an attack (on ourselves) is to become defensive, to counterattack."

"Counter antagonistic talk by soft talk," suggests Jerry Sinclair of Jacksonville, Fla. Doug Harvey is more blunt. Says he: "Two things: Voice, don't raise it. The louder he yells, the lower your voice. Plus, facial proximity. Back off and stay bland. You wrinkle your face or curl your lip and you're asking that guy to twist it some more."

Muscalus says he "can't overemphasize the importance of listening. Interpret the apparently casual remarks, look askance at apparent compliments between opponents. Hear the taunts, particularly among strong rivals, such as crosstown opponents. Every area has 'em. Locals often think they're the only ones with that vitriolic hatred. They're not; it's all over the nation."

Muscalus says that an official must be able to "read" players' responses. "The team getting trounced may be prone to turn up the heat or deflect it," notes Muscalus. "Let them turn a little fury on you. 'Don't embarrass yourselves,' I tell them. 'You've given it all you've got. Don't spoil it. Your folks and your friends in the stands will be ashamed if you let yourself go.' You get more out of them by compliments, boosting their egos."

What all this boils down to is that you can't haphazard your way through turmoil. You've got to anticipate it whenever possible, but most of the time you have to employ a concerted strategy to prevent things from escalating.

"Sometimes it's as simple as holding the whistle a few seconds before you declare the ball ready for play," offers football official Jerry Sinclair. "Once in a while you can just look a player square in the eyes and shake your head," adds Louis Vaeth, Kissimmee, Fla.

Don Rutledge, Orlando, Fla., is among the most respected men's college basketball referees today. He suggests that you might "withhold the ball just a second or two longer before handing it to a free throw shooter or on a throw-in." In baseball, Carl Childress, a veteran ump from Edinburg, Texas, says that the plate umpire could "just step around and brush the plate. You think little gestures don't count?" Another umpire, Mike Segal of Casselbury, Fla., advises that the plate ump "walk part way to the mound when tossing a new ball to the pitcher. You don't have to utter a word."

Those are little gestures, to be sure, but it also pays to have an overall plan of operation to deal with one-on-one slugfests or the occasional wild-eyed group grope around the pitcher's mound. Don Rutledge's philosophy is to "gain early control and then let the game play itself. When it seems to be heating up emotionally, tighten up the game ... and then let it go again. Let out a little string, then a little more, until the kite is flying again. Once it flies on its own, without buffeting or undue tension, let it fly."

What's important is not who is right. Not every official shares the same philosophy. What's important is to get the job done as fairly and efficiently as possible. For example, NFL referee Jerry Markbreit, from Skokie, Ill., says that he and the other NFL officials "ignore rivalries. We assume that each game will be a sharp, clean contest. These are, after all, pros. There's not likely to be any built-in ethnic or geographic antagonism." But wait a minute. No geographic sensitivity? What about Philadelphia-Pittsburgh, Chicago-Green Bay, Oakland-San Francisco and many more? "We don't even look for perennial losers to start trouble or to be

> "...gain early control and then
> let the game play itself."

extraordinarily belligerent," says Markbreit.

"That's right," says Jerry Seeman, Markbreit's boss. "Everything is positive, no hint of negativism at all." Adds Markbreit: "You go in clean, no preconceived notions. Stay upbeat. If a player shows signs of exploding, we try to compliment him, build his self-esteem. They're usually teed off because someone is beating them consistently or has made them look bad on particular plays. You need to stroke that ego."

Imagine that. Validate him as an athlete by sustaining him as a figure of substance. Build him up as a genuinely worthy person. Sounds like a mother's role, or a coach's. "When players see the officials hustling and communicating continually," continues Markbreit, "they often take their cues from that and behave accordingly."

No matter how well intentioned, no official can prevent a fight from erupting unless he gives the matter due consideration long before he steps onto any playing surface. "We should play scenes in our minds before they ever occur," says Jack Muscalus. "Offer imaginary scenarios to our crewmates to test their response. Talk through solutions before there are any problems. Remember, while you're listening and observing, there really isn't any confrontation. That comes only when you react. It's true, we have the last word, but we don't ever have to use it."

—Adapted from an original work by Jerry Grunska, Evergreen, Colo.

Chapter 7

Mental Tough'ness (n). The essential ingredient for peak performance. Here's how you find it, understand it and put it to work in your games.

MT – Mental Toughness

February 1991, Salt Lake City, Utah — Major college men's basketball referee Bobby Dibler awoke from his nap as his officiating partners entered the hotel room. The trio would in just a few hours referee the Brigham Young-Colorado State game. But as Dibler, a 20-year Division I vet, started to ready himself for the contest, he couldn't find his pants. Initially, he thought he was simply the butt of a cruel joke.

"After confronting my partners, they convinced me they didn't have my pants. I finally realized what had happened: I'd been robbed while taking my nap," recalled Dibler, who lives in El Paso, Texas. "My wallet had been taken, which included my cash and plastic. There I was faced with getting ready to go work a game and I had been robbed. Right then and there, the game was not as important to me.

Dibler, a unit manager for Procter & Gamble, admitted the experience "took (me) out of the game." Added he: "I wasn't a very

"...your brain and body operate differently when you're happy."

good referee for the first 10 or 12 minutes of that game; I missed calls. I just didn't have a good (feel for) the game. Fortunately, the game was lopsided, but the kids were penalized because of what happened to me prior to the game."

Dibler's robbery is atypical of the things that detour officials' concentration. Still, it illustrates the connection between an official's mental state of mind and his performance. Being mentally tough, having the ability to overcome adversity is what some sports psychologists call "the most important trait" for success for both athletes and officials.

What is mental toughness? Jim Loehr, a noted sports psychologist who is the director of sports science for the U.S. Tennis Association, defined it as the "ability to shut out stress, negative thoughts, doubts and fears. In short, to concentrate on the game at hand."

Loehr, whose practice is based in Bradenton, Fla., travels more than 150,000 miles each year delivering his mental-toughness message to athletes, coaches and business executives. He has worked with many of tennis' top pros and said his most dramatic success was his work with Gabriela Sabatini just months prior to her 1990 U.S. Open victory.

Although he specializes in tennis, Loehr said his principles of mental toughness apply to all phases of life, both in and out of athletics, and certainly to officiating.

"Sports officials are performers in a high-pressure arena who are constantly presented with adversity," said Loehr. "They need to make split-second decisions. For them to perform at their best, they need to be at their 'Ideal Performance State (IPS).' That means being relaxed, calm, non-threatened and confident. It's the same conditions that are necessary for players to perform their best.

"We've learned there is a specific biochemistry of emotions: That your brain and body operate differently when you're happy or challenged versus when you are angry and upset. The chemistry of negative moods blocks the body from 'maxing' out. The person who is mentally tough has learned how to effectively handle pressure."

Being able to handle pressure off the field can help you be mentally tough on the field, as well. Tim Welke, an American

League umpire, said officials need to block out outside elements as they get ready to officiate.

"There are many times when you just don't feel good but you have to go out there to do your job," noted Welke, who lives in Kalamazoo, Mich. "Day in and day out, we (major league umpires) have to deal with long flights or hotel rooms that aren't ready when we arrive. When I was younger, those little things bothered me, but I guess I've become more conditioned to deal with them.

"I've had times when my equipment didn't arrive in time to work a game and I wore uniforms that made me look like a member of the grounds crew. You've got to push that out of your mind and do your job."

Andy Van Hellemond, a retired National Hockey League referee, recalled a time when bad weather and missed flights caused him to take a train to an NHL contest and forced him to change into his officiating garb on the train.

"It had really been a long day," said Van Hellemond, of Winnipeg. "I sure wasn't mentally ready when I hit the ice. After about eight minutes of the game, I had everybody on the ice mad at me. I had this terrible empty feeling."

Van Hellemond said his lack of concentration at the beginning of the game set the stage for later problems. He explained: "I probably missed an obvious first penalty call and then I tried to catch up. The players sensed that's the way I was going to call the whole game.

"You have to be mentally ready and prepared to work. In the first few minutes you'll set the tone for how the game will be played."

Welke added that you can't allow concentration to wane near the end of a contest. "You have to work hard all nine innings," said Welke, "especially if a game is a blowout. When I broke in there might have been an occasion when I would go through the motions late in a (lopsided) game. Maybe I'd call a pitch a strike when in fact it was really a ball; it was a lack of concentration.

"You have to remember that each pitch is important to someone: To the batter, the pitcher, etc. If you concentrate on every pitch, that's what leads to consistency. Players will remember that

> "In the first few minutes you'll set the tone for how the game will be played."

> ## Exercise is one of the best techniques to attain mental toughness.

you called pitches in the first inning the same as the ninth inning."

So how can officials faced with a non-officiating crisis turn on the switch and be ready to work their assignments? Loehr said rituals can help officials shift into more ideal emotional states. Whether it's wearing the same socks, eating at the same time before every game, or listening to the same music, rituals or routines serve a purpose. "An official needs to have rituals," claimed Loehr. "The more ritualistic the performer, the better. Rituals help you ease into that special state of mind that is needed to perform well.

"Rituals are powerful triggers for creating the perfect IPS. They help in deepening concentration, turning on the 'automatic,' raising intensity, staying loose and more."

Vinnie Mauro, a former FIFA soccer referee and former U.S. Soccer director of officials, said his pregame ritual includes clearing his mind. Explained Mauro: "I try to relax as much as possible before a match. I might watch TV or read a newspaper. If something upset me earlier in the day, one thing I like to do is stop for a cup of coffee on my way to the match. I sit and have the coffee and try to clear my mind of what has happened during the day. You just can't go into a match being upset about something that happened earlier, such as a fight with your wife or girlfriend."

Mauro said having a postgame ritual is an equally important part of his repertoire.

Said Mauro: "After each match I officiate, I mentally review what went wrong in the game. I ask myself questions like, 'Did I give out too many red cards? Was it a rough game because of some calls I missed?' Self-analysis is very important to me."

Barb Kirby, among the top college softball umpires in the country, has a pregame ritual that's a bit offbeat.

"One of the relaxation techniques I like to use is looking at photos I have in an album," said Kirby, 40, from Oklahoma City. "That forces everything out of my mind. The photos bring back memories of different games or other situations and it helps me relax."

Loehr quickly added that rituals are not superstitions. Explained he: "Superstitions are something over which you have no control, rituals are yours to control. You do them because they help get you into that IPS."

Loehr said that exercise is one of the best techniques to attain mental toughness. In addition to boosting self-esteem, endurance and energy, Loehr said, "Physically fitter means mentally tougher. ... When you exercise, you are training your body to take stress and recover from it. When you're in shape, you process the stress hormones of adrenaline much better and recover faster.

"Also, we've learned that breathing slowly and deeply, from the bottom of the lungs, can shut down the panic response almost immediately. It is particularly helpful to elongate the exhalations because that's when the muscles relax."

Loehr said officials' mental preparation is just as important as physical prep, although he added that athletes and officials often do not properly address that important element of their games. A key to being mentally prepared, noted Loehr, is visualization.

"An official who is surprised is in trouble," opined Loehr. "You need to visualize as many different possible situations which can occur during a game and how you will deal with them. Doing so will help you prepare for any adversity. "What that also does is allow you to work on 'automatic.' The more you know your subject, the better off you'll be; the more confidence you'll have. Officials who think too much and try to use logic and deliberate thought will make mistakes. You have to make quick decisions, trust yourself and trust that you've done your homework."

Jim Sprenger, a Pac-10 football referee from Auburn, Wash., agreed with Loehr's assessment of shifting into automatic pilot.

"If you don't know the rules and you have to stop and think about them, you're not doing your job," said Sprenger, an insurance broker. "Being able to turn it on automatic is the only way to officiate. Having rules knowledge provides the confidence you need on the field: You're prepared to handle any situation."

"Part of my preparation is knowing the teams," added Mauro, "I like to be aware of the tactics that teams use. I try to get video of the teams to see how they play, their styles. That little extra knowledge helps me know what things to look for."

Once you've taken care of your pregame rituals and preparation, how you handle in-game situations determines another

> ## The thin line between confidence and arrogance needs to be carefully drawn.

> # "Officials have to be very careful how and when they use humor."

level of success. Explosive situations with and between players and coaches require the insertion of a calming element. In many cases, that can and should come from an official.

"The best officials project an air of confidence," noted Loehr. "They must project calmness and look calm. They can't get upset or show nervousness. An official who during a game shows those emotions is in trouble."

"An official who is angry, defensive or feels threatened will be less effective. If an official is upset, he must be able to keep that inside while on the outside he appears to be calm and in control. Players, coaches and spectators are quick to pick up on an official who is nervous or not in control."

There is a danger, however, in how an official projects himself during a contest. The thin line between confidence and arrogance needs to be carefully drawn. College football referee Sprenger called it having a "quiet confidence."

"Officials need to have a good sense of how they're coming across when they're working," said Loehr. "Are they showing confidence? Do they upset players, coaches and spectators by being too confident? Or, by being arrogant? For some, it's worth having other officials observe their work and offer assessments of how they're being perceived. "Officials need to be friendly, firm, objective and clear when they officiate. That needs to be constantly reinforced."

Another weapon officials can add to their mental-toughness arsenals is humor. Loehr said those who can laugh are in emotional control and humor offers a stress release.

"Humor, when used by an official in the proper context, is a real strength," said Loehr. "An official who can laugh or smile is in control. An official who is so uptight that he can't see the humor in a situation or can't smile is not in control.

"However, we don't want officials telling jokes. Officials are in positions of authority, and for some coaches, players and fans, officials who are laughing or smiling could convey the wrong messages. Officials have to be very careful how and when they use humor."

"There are some coaches with whom I can use humor and

others I can't," said college cage ref Dibler. "I think it's important that officials wait until they've established themselves before they use it. It has to be the right time and the right coach.

"I feel that every night there will be an opportunity to smile on the court. A pleasant smile. People always see the guy in the striped shirt as the bad guy. Hopefully, a smile helps to dispel that myth."

Mauro said humor can also be used as part of preventative officiating. "I remember a game when a player had a breakaway and missed the shot," said Mauro. "Afterward, he used a four-letter word, which I heard. I said to him: 'Hey, your mother's in the stands. What if she heard you say that word?' He chuckled and said, 'I'm sorry, ref.' He didn't direct his comment to anyone, but instead of penalizing him, I used humor and made my point."

Van Hellemond said officials are there to "defuse" situations, not ignite them, and said that humor and a tad of psychology work wonders.

"One thing I've done when I've gotten into a discussion with a player is to ask him a question," said Van Hellemond. "I've said to him, 'Do you like me?' He'll respond, 'Yes, I like you.' Then I'll say, 'Ask me if I like you.' I'll tell him that I like him and then I'll say: 'Then why are we arguing? I respect you as a player, you respect me as an official.'

"If you get the player to answer a question or two, he tends to forget what he was arguing about. If we (officials) are answering questions from players, we're on the defensive. Make the player answer some questions and not always about whether they like you. They can be questions which have to do with what might have just happened."

Softball ump Kirby recalled an exchange with an upset coach which had humorous overtones.

"In July, I was working a weekend tournament," said Kirby, who owns a landscaping business. "I was tired and having a bad game behind the plate. In the sixth inning a pitch came in that I called a ball. The coach yelled from the dugout, 'Where was that pitch, outside?' I said, 'No.' He said, 'Was it high?' I replied, 'No.' He then said, 'What was wrong with the pitch?' I said, 'Nothing.'

"The crowd began to laugh at our exchange. The coach then

> **"The use of humor when you're officiating needs to be appropriate. It needs to be subtle, gentle."**

asked, 'Did you miss the pitch?' I shot back, 'Yup.'

"The use of humor when you're officiating needs to be appropriate. It needs to be subtle, gentle."

Loehr said that having fun is another critical component of the mental-toughness equation.

"The more a person enjoys what he's doing, the more all the qualities of mental toughness will fall into place," said Loehr. "Fun really needs to dominate the experience. For officials, it's so important they look forward to their games. If an official can't carve out a sense of enjoyment in what he's doing, he won't be at his best.

"Having fun and enjoying yourself is an important element of being relaxed, calm, positively energized, unanxious and optimistic. Having fun and enjoying yourself is a highly-controllable feeling."

Once you've "mastered" the skills leading to mental toughness, it's important to remain confident, not cocky, in order to keep things in proper perspective. Van Hellemond related a procedure which has kept him humble.

Said Van Hellemond: "Early in my career, I received praise every so often for the job I did. Then further on in my career I started to question the motives for players, coaches or writers making those positive comments about me. It began to get a little too easy for me to think I was better than the next guy.

"What I then started doing was keeping all the negative things written about me. I save all those clippings and periodically read them. They bring me back to earth."

In his book *Mental Toughness Training For Sports*, Loehr wrote that mental toughness is learned, not inherited: "This is an important understanding. Very simply, if you are a mentally tough competitor, you learned to be one, and if you're not, you didn't. Mental toughness has nothing to do with your heredity, your intelligence or your character.

"Mental toughness is an acquired skill. The process through which it is acquired is precisely the same as applies to physical skills: Hard work, understanding and practice. The point is this: If you want to be mentally tougher, you can."

—Adapted from an original work by Jerry Tapp, Racine, Wis.

Chapter 8

Preparing For Your 'Big Game'

REFEREE

In his book *Mental Toughness Training For Sports*, James Loehr offers advice to athletes on preparing for their big games. Loehr said the same principles can be adapted to officials as they ready for important assignments. What can you do to improve your chances of doing your best? How should you prepare to accomplish that goal? Loehr offers these do's and don'ts.

DO stay on your regular schedule of eating, sleeping and drinking. Self-discipline is an excellent self-confidence builder.

DON'T significantly change the physical training routine that

Dress to win.

has worked best. Now is not the time for over-training.

DO spend a little time each day thinking and rehearsing how you want to perform.

DON'T wait until the night before the contest to do all your mental preparation. Cramming too much information at the last minute can overload the circuit.

DO prepare yourself mentally and physically for anything that might happen during the game; being caught by surprise may be a sign of trouble.

DON'T try to make major changes in your physical-skill level. To work your best, you need to be able to shift into cruise control, do things automatically.

DO everything you can to achieve a physical, emotional and intellectual high for the game. Avoid things that are likely to make you particularly tired, depressed, sad or upset. Avoid negative emotions.

DON'T get involved in activities, events or situations that are likely to lead to personal problems or major conflicts, which can leave you physically and emotionally drained. Staying alert, positive, energized and focused during your game may be impossible when you are emotionally spent.

DO start building momentum within yourself. Stimulate an avalanche of positive energy for yourself.

DON'T get anxious about being anxious. Don't worry about not sleeping the night before the game. Research shows that a restless night of sleep before a game usually will not hurt performance — if you don't worry about it.

DO dress to win. If you have to first put on your right shoe to feel lucky, do it. Superstition or not, if it helps, do it. Those types of things are called "dress rituals" and they are important.

DON'T eat anything substantial within two hours of game time.

DO — most importantly — have fun and enjoy yourself during the game.

— by the editors of *Referee* magazine

Chapter 9

Recipe for Success

Master chefs search for culinary combinations that tantalize the taste buds. Like Great Grandma's secret recipe for chocolate chip cookies, refereeing 'recipes,' designed to enhance officials' work, are passed down through generations. With the help of 10 contributing 'chefs,' here is one sure-fire recipe for success. Its ingredients: A dash of philosophy, a pinch of common sense and a sprinkle of communication.

The late J. Dallas Shirley was a 33-year basketball official from Reston, Va. He supervised Southern Conference men's basketball and football officials. Considered to be among the "Master Chefs" of basketball officiating, Shirley in 1980 was enshrined as an official

> "...When you provoke people, they tend to fire back. That's what you want to avoid."

in the Basketball Hall of Fame in Springfield, Mass. During his two decades as a supervisor, Shirley offered a buffet of reminder cards to interested officials. Each card, about three-by-five inches in size, contains a helpful hint that allows officials to mentally prepare for upcoming games.

Though specifically designed for basketball, his philosophies can be applied to any sport. Here is a list of J. Dallas Shirley's "ingredients," some edited for publication. The material following each item was added by author Bill Topp, who included comments from well-known officials.

CULTIVATE YOUR VOICE: FIRM. LOUD ENOUGH TO BE HEARD, NOT CHALLENGING.

Your voice can be a positive tool that helps you control a game or it can be a dagger used to knife a perceived opponent. Appropriate and timely communication is paramount to game control.

Verbal skills are exercised by all officials in all sports. One tough spot: baseball's dugouts. Throughout the course of a game, an umpire likely will hear people complaining from the dugouts, sometimes far away from home plate. Handling those people calmly yet firmly requires preparation.

Jon Bible, former national coordinator of the NCAA Umpiring Improvement Program, tries to calm things from home plate and avoids marching over to the dugout unless absolutely necessary. Said Bible: "Does that mean you have to sit there and be cussed out? No. Does that mean you've got to be shown up? No. But it does mean you don't want to appear as the aggressor. ... Say things like, 'Hey, I've heard enough.' ... When you provoke people, they tend to fire back. That's what you want to avoid."

Officiating youth games can really test one's self-control. Often times the fans and even the coaches do not understand the rules. Let's face it ... everyone is an "expert" on the game because they watch it on television. They may think they know the rules because they saw a certain play recently on television or at a major league ballpark, but chances are your youth league does not play by the same set of game rules as the professional, college or even high school programs.

It's easy for the fans to make accusations about your ability or knowledge. If you fire-back some "cute" comment or even worse — get down to their level of personal accusations, you're in big trouble!

Follow the simple gospel that all good officials preach: Ignore the fans. Exercise your communication skills need with the players, coaches and fellow officials. If the crowd becomes unruly and disrupts the game, call upon the coach to control his parents or ask the league administrator to get involved, but never confront a fan.

QUESTIONS MAY OR MAY NOT BE ANSWERED. STATEMENTS REQUIRE NO ANSWER.

Realize that often coaches are simply venting their frustrations when confronting you, usually ending their discussions quickly.

If a basketball coach says, "He's camping in the lane," what's more effective, ignoring the statement or saying to the coach, "No way; he's been fine all night"? Most of the time, ignoring a harmless statement or acknowledging it with a simple head nod ends the matter. But when you defend your position, the coach instinctively feels defensive, then goes on the offensive, continuing the debate. Being "worked" by coaches is as much a part of officiating as making judgment calls. To a point, let them talk, but don't let them influence you by intimidation.

THE MORE YOU SAY, THE LESS IT MEANS.

Rookies and veterans alike are often guilty of the "yeah, but" syndrome. When another official or a supervisor questions your mechanics or your judgment and your first utterance is, "Yeah, but," you're usually not listening. Grandma used to say, with rolling pin in hand: "Be quiet and listen. That's why you've got two ears and only one mouth." Moral of the story: You'll learn more by listening than by talking.

> "Be quiet and listen. That's why you've got two ears and only one mouth."

> ## "...the next week we spent a lot of time talking about communication."

APPEARANCE IS IMPORTANT.
BE NEAT AND SELL YOURSELF.

There is a strong correlation between your appearance and whether you're accepted as an official. Height, weight, cleanliness and body language all play roles. If you don't look like you belong on the field or court, you are likely to have more problems than an official who looks the part.

NFL referee Johnny Grier occasionally watches college football officials and reports back to a conference what he observed. One of his focal points is appearance. Said Grier: "I look at the way the guy moves on the field and appearance means a lot: The way a guy throws his flag, the way he reacts when a coach is breathing down his neck, those types of things (are important)."

EYE CONTACT IS A MUST.

All eyes must be on every play. Eye contact is an important part of communicating with your partners, yet there are countless horror stories where eye contact didn't occur, resulting in wrong calls. Ever see one basketball official signal a "block" while another tries to sell a "charge"?

Red Cashion, a retired NFL referee, offers a definitive example of the importance of eye contact: "A few years ago (in Detroit), right at the end of the half there was a play in the end zone in which there was a question whether (the pass was caught). We ruled it incomplete. As we were sitting in the dressing room at halftime, I turned to the umpire and said, 'Great call at the end of the half on the incompletion.' He said, 'I didn't have an incompletion.' I said, 'I thought I saw your signal.' He said, 'I was just showing what the back judge had because he was waving incomplete.' The back judge said, 'I wasn't waving incomplete; I was blocked out.'

"I said, 'Well, out of curiosity, who had it?' It turned out nobody had it, nobody called it. The supervisor came down and said, 'We looked at the play real close and you made a good call: He trapped it.' We were lucky to get by with that, but the communication wasn't there. As a result, the next week we spent a lot of time talking about communication. The fact that nobody saw that play knocked us down a peg."

REFEREE THE DEFENSE: GET THE ANGLE.

Even with the many TV replays and various camera angles, television cannot always get the most advantageous angle to see each play. Think the center-field camera peering in to home plate gives you a good look at the strike zone? Though it appears it does, the camera is generally located 30-50 feet to the third-base side of home plate and 20-30 feet above the ground. Angles are critical. Tony Thompson, a baseball umpire as well as baseball umpires' supervisor for the Southern, Southeastern, Atlantic Coast and Southern conferences, talked about a play at the plate when he got the correct angle to get the play right.

Explained Thompson: "It was during a game between Mississippi and Mississippi State that was televised on ESPN. A ball was hit down the left field line and the three umpires all rotated coverage. I was working first base but ended up covering the plate. The throw beat the runner there by a good five feet and there was a collision. I looked down ready to bang him out when I saw the catcher stick his hand under his chest protector to get the ball, which nobody else could see. I called the runner safe. When I got home and looked at the game (on tape), that play was shown from three angles. Finally, the third angle showed the ball under the catcher's protector."

AS THE GAME GETS HOTTER, OFFICIALS MUST BE COOLER.

No matter what level or sport you officiate, sooner or later you'll be on the proverbial "hot seat" facing an infuriated coach or player. One well-publicized series of incidents involved then-Big Ten football referee Jerry Markbreit and Ohio State's volatile coach Woody Hayes. On Nov. 20, 1971, in Ann Arbor, Mich., Markbreit, in his seventh season as a Big Ten official, and Hayes shared billing in what the official called "one of the most bizarre (incidents) in college football history."

With 1:25 left to play and Rose Bowl-bound Michigan ahead 10-7, Ohio State quarterback Donald Lamka threw an accurate pass toward receiver Dick Wakefield, who was on Michigan's 35. At the

> "You little pip-squeak! You're not gonna walk 15 yards on me!"

"When the play happened, I thought I was 100 percent right."

last second, Wolverines' safety Thom Darden leaped over Wakefield to intercept the pass. Markbreit moved to his new position downfield, signaled a Michigan first down, then turned and was face-to-face with an angry Hayes, who felt Darden should have been flagged for pass interference. Markbreit's flag flew from his pocket: Fifteen yards, unsportsmanlike conduct.

"Hayes went crazy," recalled Markbreit. "He stormed up behind me and yelled: 'You little pip-squeak! You're not gonna walk 15 yards on me! You're gonna reverse that call and we're goin' back and they're gonna get 15 for interference!' I said, 'Please leave the field, coach.' He said: 'No, dammit! I'm staying here until you make the right call!' I'd never seen a coach so angry or out of control."

After the penalty was marked off, Markbreit continued to be verbally harassed by Hayes and was unsuccessful trying to reason with the irate coach. Markbreit recalled that Hayes "yelled and threatened and called me every epithet an official has ever been called in the history of football. ... I never raised my voice or argued. I kept thinking: 'Keep your cool, Jerry. ... Don't get mad, don't use vulgarity, don't say anything that'll come back to haunt you.'"

A few moments later, Hayes, who died in 1987, had yet another tirade, this time tearing apart the down markers and hurling them onto the field. Through it all, Markbreit kept his cool, which went a long way toward helping the game conclude without further incident.

Obviously, such behavior at a youth event is not only unacceptable but intolerable. There is no place in youth sports for coaches using vulgarity or destroying property for the sake of "making a point" with an official. If a game situation becomes so volatile, don't be afraid to stop the game until calm is restored; if it can't, stop the contest entirely.

HUSTLE, YES; RUSH, NO: SET AN EVEN TEMPO.

Hustling is working hard to get into proper position and handling penalty assessment with dispatch. Rushing is overhustling, outrunning plays for the sake of breaking a sweat or showing off. Being correct becomes secondary to how you look to others. Your games will flow better if you hustle, but never rush.

Still, you must realize that no matter what you do, some games will be as smooth as new sandpaper. Don't let that deter you from working hard to do the job.

ANTICIPATE THE PLAY, NOT THE CALL.

See the whole play from beginning to end. A near-triple play in the 1992 World Series accentuates that point. In Game Three between Toronto and Atlanta, NL umpire Bob Davidson was working second base. With no outs in the top of the fourth inning, Atlanta had Deion Sanders on second base and Terry Pendleton on first as Dave Justice hit a fly ball to right-center field. Toronto center fielder Devon White made a spectacular catch, immediately throwing the ball back to the infield.

Sanders, tagging at second, was passed by Pendleton, who was called out. In the ensuing confusion, Sanders was caught in a rundown between second and third. Jays third baseman Kelly Gruber ran toward Sanders instead of throwing to second baseman Manuel Lee. Gruber then dove for Sanders to attempt a tag. Davidson ruled Sanders safe, evoking an argument.

Davidson said that "when the play happened, I thought I was 100 percent right." Later, when he saw a photo of the play, Davidson said reporters "could surmise I was wrong." Davidson couldn't see a tag, but he knows what went wrong: He didn't see the whole play. "When Gruber was chasing Sanders, I was thinking: 'He's got to make the throw. He'll never catch Sanders.'

"I broke one of the first rules they teach at umpire school: Don't take your eyes off the ball. My eyes went to Manny Lee, who was at second base. I looked at Lee just as Gruber dove. When I looked back, it appeared to me as though the glove was between the runner's feet. I called Sanders safe. Gruber jumped up right away and said, 'I tagged him.' I said, 'No you didn't.' "

WHEN THE BALL IS DEAD, BE ALIVE: ANTICIPATE WHAT MAY BE COMING NEXT.

Referee's 5/93 feature, "Things Happen," highlighted an incident that underscores why officials need to be "alive" at all times. With

> "We couldn't get between them before they started fighting."

...they were cascaded with boos and epithets.

15:20 left in a Big Ten Conference men's basketball game between Northwestern and Wisconsin, officials Art McDonald, Mike Sanzere and Ed Hightower quelled a potentially ugly brawl by reacting quickly to a violent foul.

Northwestern's Cedric Neloms flagrantly elbowed Wisconsin's Andy Kilbride, who responded with a punch as players grabbed one another. The officials and the coaching staffs reacted quickly, separating the combatants. What could have resembled a barroom brawl was squelched. The officials doled out the appropriate fouls, ejected the fighters and moved on with the game.

Sanzere, then a major college official for 14 years and still a prominent member of several major college staffs, explained what happened: "I heard the whistle and saw Artie (McDonald) had the intentional-elbow foul and I came running in toward the players. Unfortunately, we couldn't get between them before they started fighting. My first thought was to try to get the players calmed down."

After the game, both head coaches complimented the officials. Said Wisconsin coach Stu Jackson: "They (officials) handled it very professionally and did the best they could." Added Northwestern's Bill Foster: "I thought they handled it pretty well."

COURTESY WILL PAY OFF: 'THANK YOU' AND 'PLEASE' ARE OF VALUE.

In the NFL, being "pleasant" is so important to director of officiating Jerry Seeman that courtesy is virtually league mandated. Said Seeman: "I tell my people I want things put in cruise control and that's the way we'll operate. There may be players or coaches who get excited, but there better be seven people on that field who are always going to be the same. I want that atmosphere and I want us to be pleasant."

IT IS NOT WHO IS RIGHT, BUT WHAT IS RIGHT.

Prep basketball referee Tom Cline learned that valuable lesson Feb. 18, 1982, during a league championship game. The incident was detailed in *Referee's* 11/89 feature, "Nightmare: I Had Made a Terrible Mistake."

Cline, then a 25-year veteran living in Williamsport, Pa., was the trail official responsible for a last-second shot attempt. With 20 seconds left and visiting Loyalsock High School leading 40-39, Montoursville High School inbounded the ball for a game-ending challenge. The game clock was positioned on the wall behind Cline. With about 10 seconds to go, an outside shot was missed, but Montoursville got the rebound and from the paint attempted two more shots, the last one a tap that dropped through the cords. With the frantic crowd screaming, Cline was unable to hear the final horn.

After the ball went through, a swarm of fans poured from the stands onto the floor between Cline and his partner, Dick Hort, who was positioned along the baseline facing the clock. Cline was unsure about scoring the goal.

When Cline finally reached the scorer's table, he conferred with the league-assigned timer, asking what he saw. The timer said, "Tommy, I don't think the ball was tapped before the horn went off." With that, Cline said: "OK, the goal doesn't count. Loyalsock wins it." As he and Hort left the floor, they were cascaded with boos and epithets. When the dressing room door closed, Hort said: "Tom, if you had asked me for help, I'd have told you the goal was good. I saw that ball in the air after the tap and at the very same time I saw (one second) on the clock. I was looking directly at it." Said Cline: "I had made a terrible mistake."

Cline, feeling a sense of urgency to get it right, went back out onto the floor and told the scorer that an error had been made. Cline then reversed his call, granting Montoursville an apparent victory. Loyalsock later moved that game into the win column after successfully appealing Cline's decision to change his original judgment. By rule, Loyalsock was correct: Once the officials leave the court, their jurisdiction ends.

A day later talking to a local radio announcer, Cline said, "I made a terrible mistake. I should have conferred with my partner and I didn't." Added Cline: "I was certainly humbled by the experience. It was like sitting naked in a department store window during the Christmas rush. What about the kids who played that game? Some of them had been deprived, by my actions, of one of

> "...umpires everywhere would be well advised to follow Cooney's courageous example."

life's little treasures. I am sorry for that. But today, I realize that I can make a mistake and not feel guilty about it for the rest of my life, and I can hope that one of life's many lessons was in it for the kids as well."

GUTS, NOT ARROGANCE, MAKES AN OFFICIAL.

In many officials' minds, guts and Terry Cooney are synonymous. Cooney, then an AL umpire, was working behind the plate for Game Four of the 1990 AL Championship Series between Boston and Oakland. From the mound, Boston pitching ace Roger Clemens allegedly directed obscenities at Cooney, a charge Clemens denied despite replays that attested to his vulgar language. For his profanity, Clemens was ejected by Cooney. Later, commissioner Fay Vincent suspended Clemens for five games of the '91 season.

The notorious incident lead to a nationwide debate about the role of umpires and whether superstars are or should be given preferential treatment during "big" games. Cooney's display of guts and character were commendable. *Referee* received many letters concerning the incident; nearly all writers sided with Cooney. Wrote Mark Schumacher, Erie, Pa.: "With one wave of his right hand, umpire Terry Cooney did more to benefit baseball umpires than anyone before Richie Phillips (general counsel, Major League Umpires' Assn.). ... Umpires everywhere would be well advised to follow Cooney's courageous example." Noted Jerry Sheehan, from Detroit: "When a pitcher starts jawboning, the umpire has to do what Cooney did to Clemens."

Said Cooney, who retired from the AL after the 1991 season: "Wherever I go people want to know about (the Clemens' incident). Although I've tried my whole career to keep a low profile, I have been thrust into a higher profile than what I would normally like. I feel I handled (the incident) 100 percent correct and I wouldn't do anything different at all."

Blending the ingredients offered in this story will enhance your chances of becoming a "master chef" in any sport. For best results, refer often to the recipe.

—Adapted from an original work by Bill Topp, *Referee* editor

Chapter 10

Always Safe at Home

We all want to see children have fun and perform well. Especially in youth sports, kids will be kids and do things in game situations that we know is not fundamentally correct. Still, even when observing such behavior, it is not proper for the official to offer advice or suggestions. All that will get you is an angry coach and a confused player.

What youth officials can do is be positive and encourage good sportsmanship and play. Without becoming a cheerleader, if a child performs an astounding play, it is certainly okay to say so. Don't make a scene, but a word of encouragement such as, "Great catch!" or "Good try, maybe next time you'll get it!" is not only acceptable, but may make a permanent impression on that child that officials care about him or her as a person.

I remember after umpiring one season of little league ball, an eight-year-old came up to me after his last game of the season and asked me to autograph a baseball. I was really taken back by the request, "Me? An umpire?"

The father of this kid was standing nearby and he told me that his kid had, "taken a liking to me during the season because I had 'been nice to him' and had encouraged him one day when he missed a ball."

"You didn't yell at him." the father said, "You told him it was OK and he'd catch the next one. He remembered that all year long."

I didn't remember the specific incident, but this event reinforced in my own mind how important my purpose as a role-model for the kids was in the league. So, I signed his baseball with these words of encouragement: "You're always safe at home!"

As adults we often forget how one word or expression can make the difference in a person's day. Many children never receive the simple praise needed to help them build confidence. Here are a few encouraging words that you can share when the time is right:

• Wow • Way to go • Super • That's an MVP play • You're special • Outstanding • Excellent • Great • Good • Neat • Well done • Remarkable • I knew you could do it • I'm proud of you • Fantastic • Super star • Nice work • Looking good • Super Play • Great catch • That will make your coach proud • You're on top of it • Beautiful • Now you're flying • You're catching on • Incredible play • Bravo • You're fantastic • Hooray for you • You're on target • You're on your way • How nice • How smart • Good job • That's incredible • Hot dog • Dynamite • Beautiful job • You're doing great • Nothing can stop you now • Good for you • You're a winner • Remarkable job • Beautiful work • Spectacular • You're spectacular • Keep on trying • Great job • You've discovered the secret • You figured it out • Fantastic job •

> ## "You're always safe at home!"

Hip, hip hooray • Bingo • Magnificent • Marvelous • Terrific • You're important • Phenomenal • You're sensational • Super work • You look like a real pro • Creative job • Applause • Super job • Excellent job • Exceptional performance • You're a real trooper • You are responsible • You're exciting • That's being a leader • You learned it right • What an imagination • What a good listener • You're fun • You're growing up • You tried hard • You care • Beautiful sharing • Outstanding performance • You're a good friend • I trust you • You're important • Don't quit • You belong • You've got a friend • You make me laugh • You brighten my day • I respect you • That's correct • You're a joy to watch • You're a treasure • You're A-OK • You made my day • That's the best • A big hug • Great effort • Good sport • Great shot • Great tackle • Great hit • Give them a big smile

— by Bob Still, National Association of Sports Officials

Chapter 11

Using Self-Evaluation to Enhance Your Work

Having both the ability and willingness to self-evaluate are critical components of improving your officiating. Regardless of sport or level, you must be able to critique yourself and be critiqued by others to maximize your abilities.

Ed Hochuli has been an NFL official since 1990, working as a referee since 1992, when he moved from back judge. He joined the NFL after 10 years of major college work, including seven in the

Pac-10. Full time, he is a civil-trial attorney who is a partner with a Phoenix law firm.

Hochuli made a presentation during the 1993 Orlando convention sponsored by the National Association of Sports Officials. His topic: self-evaluation. He said that to get more from your abilities, start by taking an honest look at yourself. "We need to understand and recognize our shortcomings," said Hochuli.

Overweight? Don't study the rules enough? Quick temper? Too technical? Once you identify the areas needing work, that process begins. "You can't run away from your problems once you recognize them," said Hochuli.

Striving to improve includes more than a philosophy; it's having a good attitude. Jerry Seeman, NFL director of officiating, is adamant that while "perfection is impossible, excellence is not. Excellence is what you get when you strive for perfection."

Bottom line: You must want to improve before you can improve.

Said Hochuli: "If you believe there is no room for improvement, get out of officiating because the next step is an obvious decline. That is embarrassing to you and your fellow officials. Every year, I am less content with my own abilities. I see so many great officials and I realize how many things I have to work on."

For a time, Hochuli observed officials at local prep and small college football games. When he talked with them after their games, one theme was consistent: The best officials focused on what they did wrong. "Their attitude was, 'I have a lot to learn,'" said Hochuli.

Once you've figured out you need to learn, it's much easier to start learning. Practice. When you're done, practice some more. For his first two years in the NFL, Hochuli was on referee Howard Roe's crew. Hochuli said that before every game, Roe stood before a mirror, practicing signals. One day, Hochuli jokingly asked Roe if he'd finally gotten them down pat. Roe turned and answered seriously, "It's important to get it just right."

Studying rulebooks and corrected exams lead to marked improvement. If rules are your nemesis, a common problem for newer officials, get after them and focus. Hochuli said that the rulebook is "the one aspect of officiating that is strictly mechanical. If you put in the time, you can teach yourself rules."

Also study mechanics. It's not enough to know where you should stand; you must know why you stand there. You won't find most of those answers within the pages of books.

The best officials focused on what they did wrong.

Philosophies are handed down from one generation to another. So, ask philosophy questions of other officials, who may offer varying answers. Try some of the approaches and incorporate into your games the ones you believe will work for you.

Hochuli said one way to improve by self-evaluation is to keep an officiating diary. After each game, write down the things you did well and the things you need to work on. Be brutally honest with yourself, as no one else has to see it. "The nice thing about a diary is that you can go back and review it before the next game or the next season," said Hochuli. When you are seen by other officials, ask for criticisms and accept them. "You're never too qualified to improve," said Hochuli. "Being picky pays off."

— by the editors of *Referee* magazine

Chapter 12

Seven Simple Tips to Success

Throughout this book we've shared with you "tried and true" solutions to problems you will face as an official — regardless of the level.

However, now it's time to summarize youth-sports officiating and we've done so with Seven Simple Tips to Success ...

KEEP YOUR PERSPECTIVE.

Right now your most important goal is being a good official for your youth sports program. By studying, observing and practicing you will improve, just as the kids do when they practice.

Remember, it's a game for the kids. Help them have fun.

PREPARE FOR THE UNEXPECTED.

Take time before each game to talk with your partners about responsibilities. Meet at least 15 minutes prior to the start of your game and go over the local ground rules, any special interpretations or concerns that might exist about the teams involved. Don't leave any doubts unresolved with your partner.

REMEMBER, YOU'RE IN CHARGE.

We just said it a few paragraphs ago. Youth sports is for the kids. When dealing with coaches or parents who can't control themselves in front of the children, you do not have to "take it" as much as officials at other levels. There are ways to handle verbally abusive coaches, players and fans.

Be up front with coaches and let them know that because children are involved, abusive language and behavior will not be tolerated. Being disrespectful to an official is not part of the learning curve!

Remove disrespectful children immediately. Talk to the coach, but don't tolerate cussing or rude behavior from anyone.

Study your leagues policies carefully. When parents lose control, place the burden of crowd control on the coaches and league administrators. If they can't control the parents and fans, simply stop the contest and let league officers sort out the problem.

SAFETY FIRST.

As an official, you have a responsibility to ensure that all games are conducted in a safe environment. Do not let a coach intimidate you into beginning or continuing a game when rain, fog, lightning, wet floors, leaking roofs or other problem conditions exist. Regardless of how "important" the game might be, a liability suit naming you as a defendant has a much greater and longer lasting effect.

When in doubt, use common sense and err on the side of safety.

CLIMB THE LADDER AT YOUR OWN PACE.

Youth sports needs officials. If you become a good youth official, there will be opportunities to work high school junior varsity and varsity level games someday — if you want.

It's up to you just how far you want to go. Just go at a pace that makes you comfortable.

When in doubt, use common sense.

KEEP YOUR FOCUS.

Your opportunities in youth sports will vary, sometimes during the same day. It is not uncommon for a youth official to work a tee ball game, then do an 11- and 12-year-old baseball game.

Don't lose your focus. Remember, with each age level increase, the games become more competitive and the skill levels improve. Still, kids will be kids and mistakes of every kind can happen. You must be able to concentrate. Know that if you're not focused, you risk losing control of the game.

HUMBLE THYSELF.

No matter how good you think you are, you're only as good as your last call. Once your game is over, it's history. You should learn from it and take those lessons with you to the next game.

— by Bob Still, National Association of Sports Officials

Smart Moves
For Sports Officials!

Each booklet features 19 tips for working a better game — game-tested tips you will use no matter what level you work

19 Smart Moves
For The Baseball Umpire

Includes tips on handling pregame meetings, ejections, forfeits, incident reports, arguments and more! Written by Ken Allan, veteran NCAA Division I baseball umpire. (24-page booklet) **BSMBA, $2.95, NASO-Member Price: $2.35**

19 Smart Moves
For The Basketball Official

Includes tips on handling coaches and players, pregame meetings, technicals, game reports and more! Written by Bill Topp, *Referee* editor, author of *Basketball Officials Guidebook — Mechanics For a Crew of Two Officials,* and veteran high school and college basketball official. (24-page booklet) **BSMBB, $2.95, NASO-Member Price: $2.35**

19 Smart Moves
For The Football Official

Includes tips on handling pregame meetings, signaling, reporting penalties, maintaining game control and more! Written by Jeffrey Stern, *Referee* associate editor, author of *Football Officials Guidebook — Mechanics For Crews of Four and Five Officials,* and veteran high school and college football official. (24-page booklet) **BSMFB, $2.95, NASO-Member Price: $2.35**

19 Smart Moves
For The Soccer Official

Includes tips on communication with coaches, players and partners, positioning, appearance, stretching, start technique and more! Written by Carl P. Schwartz, author of *Soccer Officials Guidebook For a Crew of Three Officials (Diagonal System of Control)*, and veteran high school, college and USSF soccer official. (24-page booklet) **BSMSO, $2.95, NASO-Member Price: $2.35**

19 Smart Moves
For The Softball Umpire

Includes tips on game preparation, pregame meetings, fair/foul coverage, gray-area mechanics, making pivots, managing arguments and more! Written by Jay Miner, *Referee* contributing editor, softball columnist and veteran umpire. (24-page booklet) **BSMSB, $2.95, NASO-Member Price: $2.35**

Associations:
Make the *19 SMART MOVES ...* booklets part of your group's training materials! Save up to 50% using *Referee's* group sales discounts:

1 – 9 copies	$2.95 each
10 – 24	$2.07 each
25 – 49	$1.92 each
50 – 99	$1.77 each
100 – 249	$1.62 each
250+	$1.48 each

Qty.	Order code	Description	Price	NASO Price	Amount
	BSMBA	19 Smart Moves For The Baseball Umpire	$ 2.95	$ 2.35	
	BSMBB	19 Smart Moves For The Basketball Official	$ 2.95	$ 2.35	
	BSMFB	19 Smart Moves For The Football Official	$ 2.95	$ 2.35	
	BSMSO	19 Smart Moves For The Soccer Official	$ 2.95	$ 2.35	
	BSMSB	19 Smart Moves For The Softball Umpire	$ 2.95	$ 2.35	

Shipping/Handling Chart

Up to $5	$ 2.00
$ 5.01-$ 15	$ 4.00
$ 15.01-$ 30	$ 6.00
$ 30.01-$ 50	$ 8.00
$ 50.01-$ 70	$10.00
$ 70.01-$100	$12.00
$100.01-$250	$15.00
Over $250	CALL FOR RATE

RESIDENTS OUTSIDE 48 CONTIGUOUS STATES:
CALL 800/733-6100 FOR SHIPPING RATES.

Subtotal

Wisconsin residents add 5% sales tax

Shipping & Handling (see chart)

TOTAL

Name _____ Address _____

City, State, Zip _____ Daytime Phone _____

Referee/NASO Account # _____

❑ Check/Money order ❑ MasterCard ❑ VISA

Account # _____ Expiration Date _____

Signature _____
(required only if using credit card)

101Y

Notes

Notes